CAMBRIDGE PRIMARY
English
Phonics Workbook

B

My name is ....

I am .... years old.

I go to .... School.

Gill Budgell and Kate Ruttle

CAMBRIDGE
UNIVERSITY PRESS

CAMBRIDGE
UNIVERSITY PRESS

University Printing House, Cambridge CB2 8BS, United Kingdom

One Liberty Plaza, 20th Floor, New York, NY 10006, USA

477 Williamstown Road, Port Melbourne, VIC 3207, Australia

314–321, 3rd Floor, Plot 3, Splendor Forum, Jasola District Centre, New Delhi – 110025, India

103 Penang Road, #05-06/07, Visioncrest Commercial, Singapore 238467

Cambridge University Press is part of the University of Cambridge.

It furthers the University's mission by disseminating knowledge in the pursuit of education, learning and research at the highest international levels of excellence.

www.cambridge.org
Information on this title: www.cambridge.org/9781107675926

First published 2015

20 19 18 17 16

Printed in Italy by Rotolito S.p.A.

A catalogue record for this publication is available from the British Library

ISBN 978-1-107-67592-6 Paperback

Contents

Trace the letters here. Say the sounds aloud.

sh   th   ch   ng   nk

Write the words under the pictures.

cat

Draw and write a word
ending with **sh**.

Draw and write a word
beginning with **ch**.

Write a word from the box to finish each sentence.

The _____ is cross. He has a mark on his _____ .

sing
king
wing

chin
chip
shin

Thin
Them
This

" _____ is not good."

"Rub it _____ a _____ . Look it is off."

this
with
them

chip
chick
cloth

To read this word,
say c-l-o-th

" _____ a lot of fuss!"

Rich
Much
Such

Think
Thank
Thick

" _____ you."

Trace the letters here and say the sounds aloud.

Say these as a long sound like **moon**.

ai ee ie oa oo oo

Finish the crossword. Use the picture clues.
Write one letter in each box.

Say these as a short sound like **book**.

Write the words again here.

ai _____   oa _____

ee _____   oo (short) _____

ie _____   oo (long) _____

Write **yes** or **no** in each box to answer the questions.

Is the sheep in the road?

Will the big man get his foot in the boot?

Is my pie on my spoon?

Can we sail a boat?

Trace the letters here and say the sounds aloud.

oi ow ar or ir er

Look at each picture. Say the word aloud.
Draw lines to match each word to its picture.

fork

jar

bird

cow

oil

crown

girl

flower

Finish the words under the pictures.

sh ____ k	sh ____ t	____ l
st ____	c ____ n	____ m
sk ____ t	c ____	c ____ k

Trace the letters here and say the sounds aloud. A line between letters shows where a letter is missing.

ai   a_e   ay

Underline all the words in each sentence with **ai**, **a_e** or **ay**.

Jane came for a play day.

She came to play games with me.

First, we had a race.

Then we went sailing in the rain.

Then we made cakes with Mum.

We had a good play day.

Write two of the words in each box.

Words with **ai**	Words with **a_e**	Words with **ay**

The mixer machine makes each set of letters into a proper word.
Write the words the machine will make. The first letter of each word is
underlined. A line between letters shows a letter is missing there.

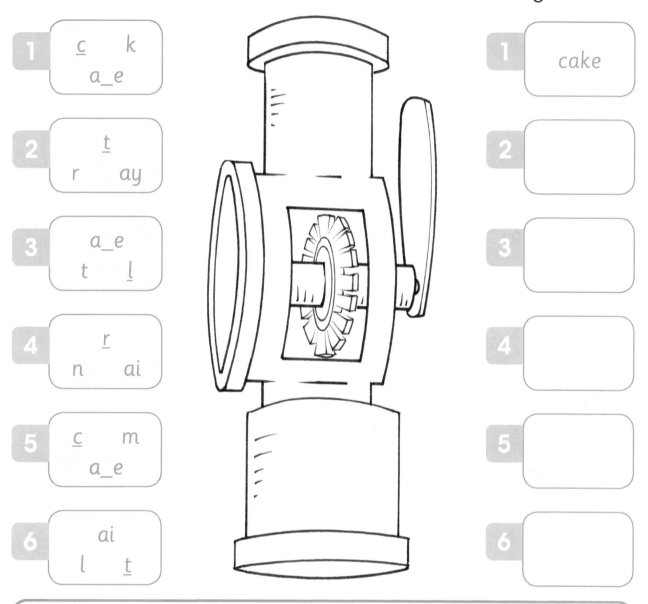

1   c̲   k
     a_e

1   cake

2   t̲
  r   ay

2

3   a_e
  t   l̲

3

4   r̲
  n   ai

4

5   c̲   m
     a_e

5

6   ai
  l   t̲

6

Read these words aloud. Trace the words here.

came made make
today always

Trace the letters here and say the sounds aloud.

ee ee ee ea ea ea

Draw a ring around all the things in this picture that
have the sound **ee** or **ea** like in **eat**.

ee

ea

ee ee ee ea ea ea

Colour the pictures green if they have an **ee** (**ea**) sound. Then write **ee** or **ea** next to the picture.

Read the word **please**. Trace the word.

please

Read the word **people**. Trace the word.

people

Read the sentence.
Please make these people go away.

Trace the letters here and say the sounds aloud.

ie   i_e   igh   y

Read the words and draw pictures in the boxes.

bike	night	tie
light	ride	fly

Write the words here.

ie	i_e	igh	y

Read the words aloud.
Trace the words here.

by   *my*   *like*

time   *might*

Write one of the words in each gap below.

It is _____ for bed.

I _____ need you to read

_____ book.

I _____ it when you are asleep

_____ nine o'clock.

Now go to sleep.
Good night.

Trace the letters here and say the sounds aloud.

Say this like the sound in **slow**.

oa   o_e   ow   oe

Finish the crossword. Use the picture clues.
Write one letter in each box.

Write the words again here.

oa	o_e	oe	ow

Trace the letters here and say the sounds aloud.

oa   o_e   ow   oe

Choose letters from the boxes and then finish the words.

oa

o_e

b _____

o_e

oa

c _____

oe

ow

win _____

oe

ow

_____

Read the word at the beginning of each line. Then ring all the words that are the same on that line.

don't   do   dont   don't   dont'   don't

old   do   old   low   don't   old   do   old

so   do   to   so   go   so   of   so   no   so

Trace the letters here and say the sounds aloud.

oo ue u_e ew ◄ Long sounds

Short sounds ► u oo

Underline all the words in each sentence with **oo**, **ue**, **u_e**, **ew**, **oo** and **u**.

In my dream ...
I put on my new blue boots.

I grew wings. The wind blew
and I flew up to the moon.
I played good tunes on a flute.

Then my wings came off and
I fell into a bush. I stood up and
shook myself ... and then I woke up.

Write three words with a long **oo** sound. oo, ue, u_e, ew	Write three words with a short **oo** sound. oo, u

The mixer machine makes each set of letters into a proper word.
Write the words the machine will make. The first letter of each word
is underlined.

1 s   n
        oo

2   oo
   t   k

3   u
   t   p

4   g
   r   ew

5 b   u
      sh

6   ue
   l   b

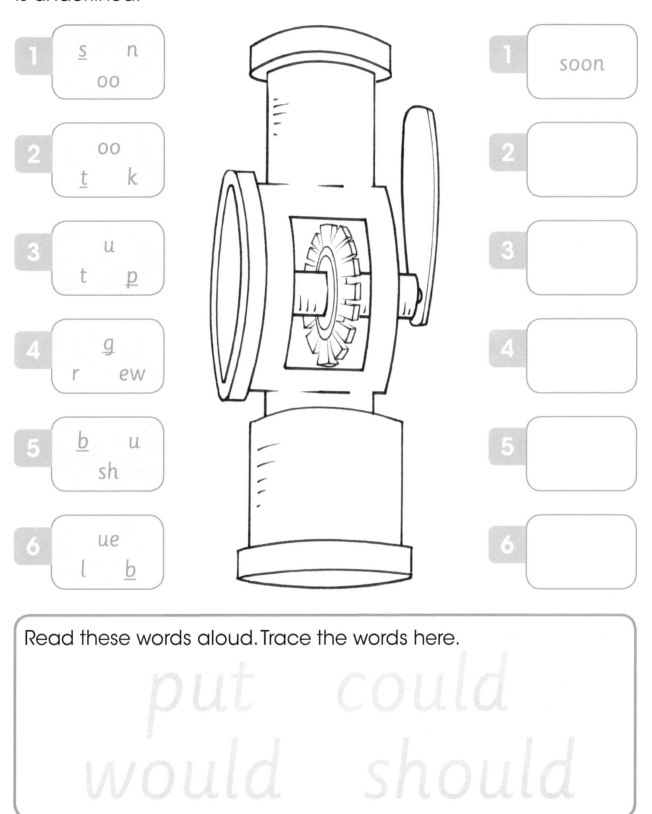

1 soon

2

3

4

5

6

Read these words aloud. Trace the words here.

put   could

would   should

Trace the letters here and say the sounds aloud.

ar ir ur
or aw ore

Look at each picture. Say the word aloud.
Draw lines to match each word to its picture.

bark

burn

bird

saw

store

sport

Finish the words under the pictures.

g _____ l

sn _____

sh _____ k

h _____ t

s _____

f _____ k

Read these words aloud: **are   your   saw   more**

Write the words here:

are your

saw more

Write one of the words in each gap below:

We s_____ y_____ teacher.

We _____ not happy.

You must do _____work.

Trace the letters here and say the sounds.

ow ou oi oy

Say this like the sound in **now**.

Draw lines to join each word to its picture.

owl

mouse

cloud

shout

boy

coin

soil

enjoy

Write two **ou** or **ow** words and three **oi** or **oy** words from the picture in these boxes:

ou or **ow**

oi or **oy**

Trace the letters here and say the sounds aloud.

ow ou oi oy

Draw lines to join each spelling to its picture.

ow ou

oi oy

Sound out a-b-ou-t   ou-r
Read the words aloud: about   our

Trace the words here.

about   our

Sound out e-n-j-oy   Read the word aloud: enjoy

Trace the word here.

enjoy

Read the sentence.
We are about to enjoy our meal.

Trace the letters here and say the sounds aloud.

air → are ear ←

eer ear

Say this like the sound in **share**.

Say this like the sound in **wear**.

Say this like the sound in **near**.

Read the words and draw the pictures in the boxes.

chair	bear	stare

ear	deer	cheer

Read the words aloud. Trace the words here.

there   their

dear   near

Write one of the words in each sentence below.

_____ Grandpa.

We are camping.
_____ are bears _____
our tent.

They like my food as well
as _____ own food.

They scare me a bit, but they
do not hurt us.

From Jen

Trace the letters here and say the sounds aloud.

f ff ph w wh

Finish the crossword. Use the picture clues.
Write one letter in each box.

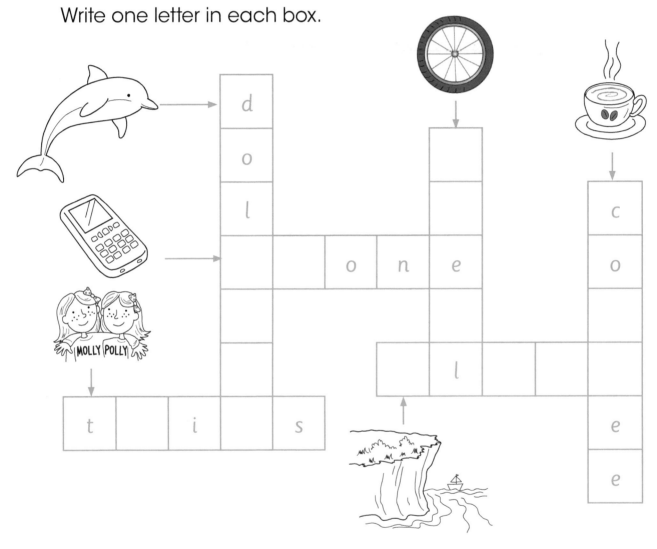

Ring the pairs of letters which make one sound.

Trace the letters here and say the sounds aloud.

f f ff ph w wh

Choose letters from the boxes and then finish the words.

w

wh

_____ indow

w

wh

_____ ale

f

ph

_____ otograph

ff

ph

sni _____

Read the word at the beginning of each line. Ring all the words that are the same on the line.

where   there   where   were   where

when   then   when   them   when   when

Revision

Write the words in the boxes under the pictures.

Read the words aloud: **some one**
Trace the words here.

some   one

Read the questions. Write **yes** or **no** for each answer.

Is your new coat white? _____

Will he use a saw to cut some wood for his fire?

_____

Do stars shine at night? _____

If I glue these bits, will I make a boat?

_____

The same letter can make different sounds in different words.
We can say the letters **a** and **e** in different ways.

Write **a** or **e** to finish each word. Read each **a** word with one of these sounds: **a, ay, o** or **ar**. Read each **e** word with one of these sounds: **e, i**.

_____pple

b_____by

sw_____n

ban_____na

_____leven

_____gg

h_____n

bask_____t

Draw red rings around the things in the picture that are words with **e** in them, and black rings around the things in the picture that are words with **a** in them.

Look at the words next to the picture.

Find a word where **a** makes an 'ay' sound (like **day**) _____

Find a word where **a** makes an 'ar' sound (like **star**) _____

Find a word where **a** makes an 'o' sound (like **hot**) _____

Find a word where **e** makes an 'i' sound (like **sit**) _____

Draw lines to join the pictures where the underlined letters sound the same.

banana

watch

elephant

hop

insect

car

Read the words aloud: **want**   **what**

Trace the words here.

want what

Read the words aloud: **ask**   **after**

Trace the words here.

ask   after

Read the sentence.
Ask what we want to do after this.

The same letter can make different sounds in different words. We can say the letters **i** and **y** in different ways. Look at each picture. Say the word aloud.
Draw lines to match each word to its picture.

insect

lion

child

blind

pilot

yes

baby

lorry

Finish the words under the pictures using letters **i** or **y**.

l_____on

grann_____

ch_____ld

lorr_____

p_____lot

bab_____

Read the words aloud: **very   suddenly**

Trace the words here.

very   suddenly

Write one of the words in each gap below.

That is a _____ wild lion.

_____ it roared _____ loudly.

We can say the letters **O** and **U** in different ways.
Finish the crossword. Use the picture clues. Write **O** or **U** in each box.

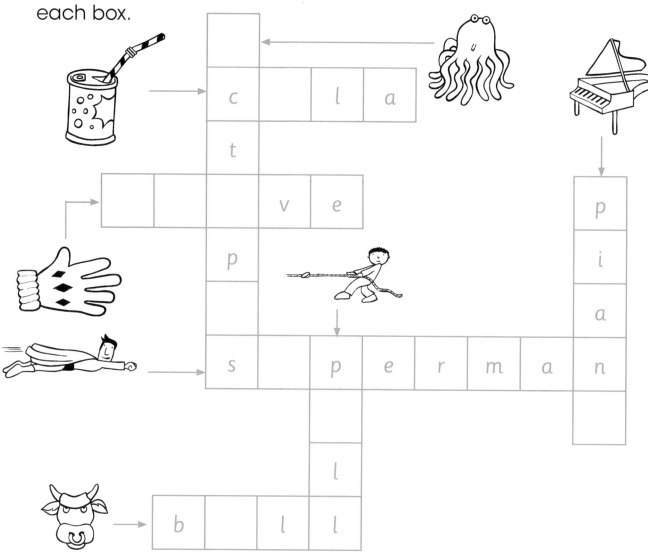

Write the words again here.

Words with o	Words with u

Choose letters from the boxes to finish each word.

o

u

cl_____thes

o

u

m_____ther

o

u

p_____st

o

u

f_____ll

Read the words aloud.
over   only   one   some   other

Trace the words here.

over   only   one
some   other

The same letters can make different sounds in different words.
We can say the letters **ie** and **ea** in different ways.
Underline all the words in each sentence with **ie** and **ea**.

The eagle cleans its feathers with its beak.

It sees some children having a picnic in a field.

The eagle sees some pie.

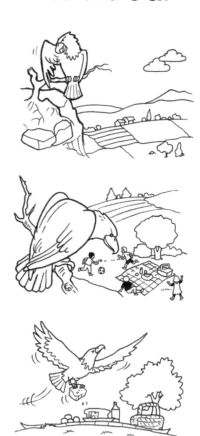

With a loud shriek, it grabs a piece of pie.
The thief!

Sort the words into these boxes.

Words where ea sounds like *bead*	Words where ea sounds like *head*	Words where ie sounds like *lie*	Words where ie sounds like *chief*

The mixer machine makes each set of letters into a proper word.
Write the words the machine will make.

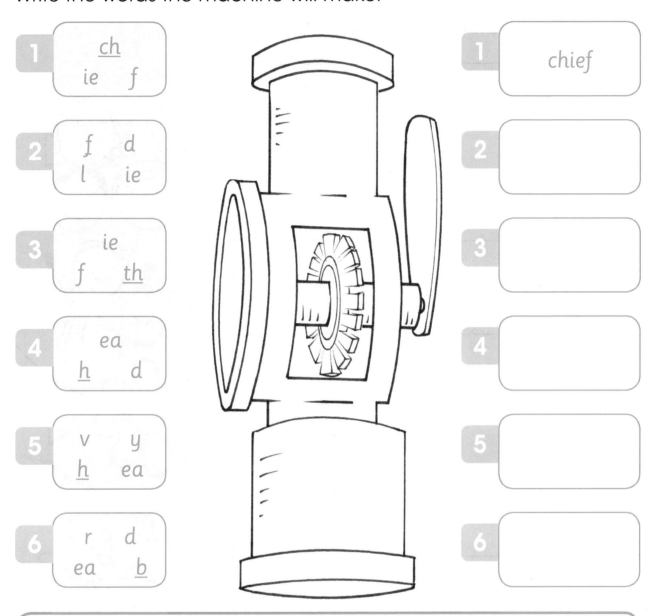

1	ch ie f		1	chief
2	f d l ie		2	
3	ie f th		3	
4	ea h d		4	
5	v y h ea		5	
6	r d ea b		6	

Try to sound out these words. Read them aloud. Then trace them here.

friend   each
really   easy

We can say the letters **OW** and **OU** in different ways.
Read the words below and find the matching pictures. Then draw your own pictures in the boxes.

arrow

flower

mouse

shoulders

soup

group

Read the questions. Write **yes** or **no** for each answer.

Do you follow your shadow?

_____

Can you run about in the playground?

_____

Did she throw the ball over her shoulder?

_____

Do you use a pillow when you have a shower?

_____

We can say **c** and **g** in different ways. Finish the crossword. Use the picture clues. Write one letter in each box.

Write a word with **c** like in **cat**. _____

Write a word with **c** like in **city**. _____

Write a word with **g** like in **girl**. _____

Write a word with **g** like in **age**. _____

Choose letters from the boxes to finish each word.

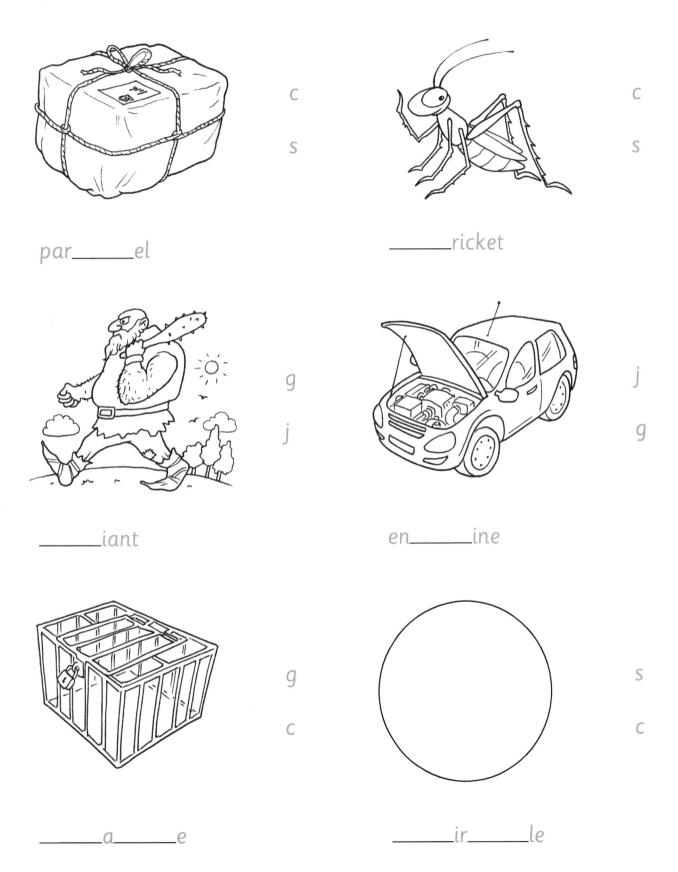

par_____el

c

s

_____ricket

c

s

_____iant

g

j

en_____ine

j

g

_____a_____e

g

c

_____ir_____le

s

c

Revision

Read the words.

Then draw the pictures in the boxes.

giraffe	rainbow	gloves	head
lion	pencil	engine	soup
heavy	bull	lorry	circle
dancer	friends	feathers	swan

Read the words below aloud then trace them here.

even   ever

Read the questions. Write **yes** or **no** for each answer.

Do you ever dance in the bath?

_____

Can you count to one thousand?

_____

Do giraffes have feathers?

_____

Has the chicken lost her scarf?

_____

The letter **S** can make different sounds in different words. Draw lines to join each word below to its picture.

castle

whistle

horse

mouse

nose

ears

present

cheese

Write three words here with the same sound as **sister** and **fuss**.	Write three words here with the same sound as **visitor** and **zoom**.

Draw lines to join the pictures where the underlined
letters sound the same.

house

sneeze

noise

castle

glass

buzz

Try to sound out the word: **p-l-ea-se**   Read the word: **please**

Trace the word.

please

Try to sound out the word: **l-i-st-en**   Read the word: **listen**

Trace the word.

listen

Read the sentence.

Please listen and I will tell you what we are going to
do next.

Read the words and draw the pictures in the boxes.
Hint: the underlined letters make a 'sh' sound.

sugar	station	ocean

Hint: the underlined letters make a 'zh' sound.

television	treasure	measure

Hint: the underlined letters make a 'ch' or a 'j' sound.

picture	bridge	edge

Underline all the sounds which are like the
underlined sounds in **<u>sh</u>ip**, **<u>ch</u>ip**, **<u>g</u>iant** or **plea<u>s</u>ure**.

I saw a strange creature
on the television.

It was like a mixture
of a dragon and a sheep.

I drew a special picture of it.
It was having an adventure.
It took me ages to draw.

I gave my picture to Mum.
As usual, she put it in her
treasure chest.

Sort the words from the story into these boxes.

Words with a sound like <u>sh</u>ip	Words with a sound like <u>ch</u>ip	Words with a sound like <u>g</u>iant	Words with a sound like plea<u>s</u>ure
	creature	strange	

Review your learning. There are different ways of spelling the
sounds **ai**, **ee**, **ie** and **oa**. Choose letters from each box to
finish the words.

ai

a_e

sn_____k_____

ee

ey

donk_____

ee

y

Mumm_____

y

ie

cr_____

ow

oe

sn_____man

ea

ee

sh_____p

Finish the crossword. Use the picture clues. Write one letter in each box.

Write the words from the crossword here.

Words with vowel sounds like **rain**	Words with vowel sounds like **feet**	Words with vowel sounds like **pie**	Words with vowel sounds like **soap**

There are different ways of spelling long **oo**, **or**, **ir** and **ar** sounds.
Read the words below and draw the pictures in the boxes.

comp<u>u</u>ter	w<u>al</u>k	p<u>al</u>m tree
<u>Ea</u>rth	<u>f</u>our	res<u>cu</u>e
s<u>ear</u>ch	w<u>or</u>m	d<u>au</u>ghter

Read the story. Underline the words in the story that have sounds like **oo**, **or**, **ir** or **ar**.

There are worms in the earth in
our garden. If you cut them in half,
they grow again.
I like to talk to the worms.

You have to get up early and
search for them. Sometimes
the birds eat them.

If you stand as still as a statue,
the birds come quite close.

Once a bird caught a worm.
I threw a tissue at it and the bird
dropped the worm and flew away.

Write two words you underlined in the story in these boxes.

oo sound	or sound
ir sound	**ar sound**

Look at each picture. Say the word aloud.
Draw lines to match each word to its picture.

flower

zebra

colour

theatre

camera

caterpillar

visitor

father

All these words end in the same sound. Draw a ring around the letters that show the last sound in each word.

Finish the words under each picture.
Choose from **er**, **ar**, **re** and **a**.

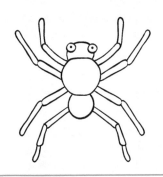

spid _____

sug _____

whisp _____

trous _____ s

fi _____

pand_____

Read these words aloud: **water   other**
Trace them here.

water   other

Write one of the words in each gap below.

Please pour some _____ into the _____ cups.

Revision

Read the words aloud. Then draw the pictures in the boxes.

horse	cheese	castle	nose
treasure	sugar	cushion	station
cage	escape	honey	sky
computer	world	four	learn

Read the questions. Write **yes** or **no** for each answer.

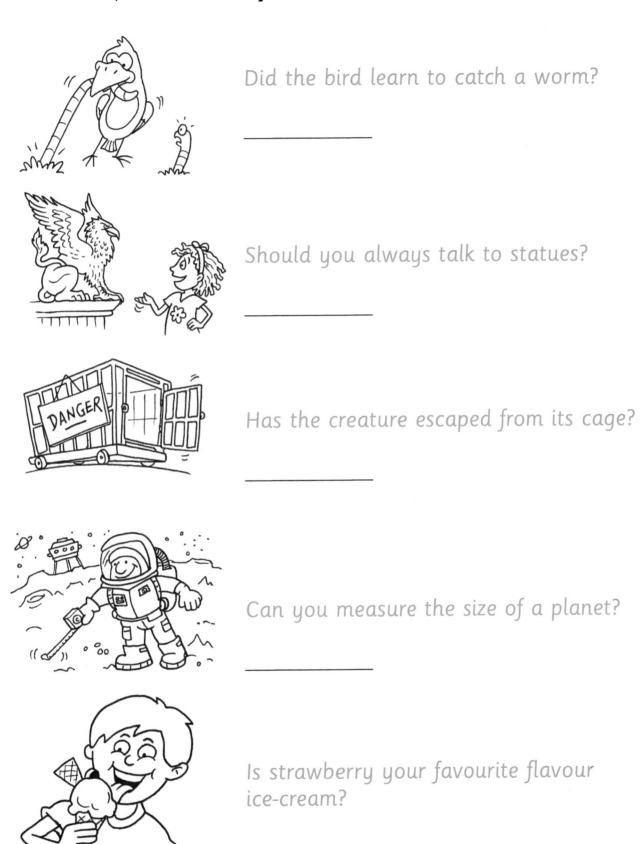

Did the bird learn to catch a worm?

_____

Should you always talk to statues?

_____

Has the creature escaped from its cage?

_____

Can you measure the size of a planet?

_____

Is strawberry your favourite flavour ice-cream?

_____

Phonics is an important skill to learn in the early stages of reading and writing. This book is intended to be used by learners who already know:

- the sounds represented by all of the letters of the alphabet.
- one sound represented by the two letters (digraphs) **sh, ch, th, ai, ee, ie, oa, ue, ar, or, ir, ou** and **oi** and the three letters (trigraphs) **ear** and **air**.
- how to **blend** known letters and digraphs to read an unknown word.
- how to **segment** a word into its sounds to spell it.

If your learners are not secure with this, they will benefit from revisiting *Phonics Workbook A*.

Phonics Workbook B introduces:
- new ways of representing the sounds already known.
- the new sound /zh/ as in trea<u>s</u>ure.
- new ways of pronouncing some familiar letter patterns.
- using familiar letter patterns when reading longer words.
- the meanings of the words 'vowel' and 'consonant'.

If you are working with learners for whom English is a second language, make sure that the vocabulary used on each page is familiar to them. These workbooks do not use the International Phonetic Alphabet (IPA) which gives symbols instead of letter patterns. Where a sound is represented by letters which may not be used to spell it, these marks // are used around the letters – for example **/ks/** for the sound of the letter **x**.

Letter names and letter sounds

When using this book, learners will need to know letter names (for example, **a = ay, b = bee, c = cee**) as well as their sounds (for example, **b = b**^{uh}, **f = fff, g = g**^{uh}). When you help a learner to hear the sounds in a word for reading or spelling, say the sounds you hear, for example, **l-igh-t** = light.

  Encourage them to continue to use 'phonic fingers' to show the sounds in a word. They should hold up one finger to represent each sound, then sweep the index finger of their other hand across

all of the fingers which are held up and say the whole word, for example, **l-igh-t** = light.

Using this workbook

Continuing the approach in *Phonics Workbook A*, the activities in *Phonics Workbook B* are intended to follow an introductory session which you do with the learners using objects, pictures and cards showing letters and letter patterns that they can manipulate. You will find it useful to have sets of card showing all familiar letters (single, double, triple) for sounds learned so far. As new letter combinations for known sounds are introduced make cards for them too. A split digraph is when two letters, for example **a** and **e**, make a sound together but are split within a word, for example *make*. When introducing split digraphs, leave a space on the card that is wide enough to insert other single letter cards.

Encourage the learners to use the cards:
- in practical activities, placing cards next to pictures or objects.
- in sorting activities, where you ask the learners to make sets of pictures, objects and letter patterns which all have the same sound.
- to create new words by combining cards. This allows learners to reinforce their understanding of the sounds in words and the sounds represented by each of the new letter patterns as flashcards, so that when you show them a sequence of letters, for example, **igh**, they respond with the sound it represents.
- in games. Play snap and memory games using sets of the cards. Encourage the learners to recognise pairs of letter patterns that represent the same sound, for example, **ie** and **igh**.

Introducing new ways of representing letter sounds

The activities on pages 10–29 and pages 44–55 are intended to build on learners' existing knowledge about how to represent a letter sound. Making choices about which letter pattern to use is the beginning of learning how to spell. The aim of this workbook is simply to introduce new combinations of letters that represent sounds, primarily for reading, so that learners are familiar with them. Spelling lessons in future years will help them to learn which choices to make and this idea is introduced in the revision lesson.

When introducing new letter combinations:
- always start from what is already known, so begin by revising the familiar letter combinations that represent the target sound.
- start working orally, using pictures, objects and letter pattern cards, saying the sounds in words, before showing the learners the new letter pattern. This helps them to associate the letter patterns with representative pictures and objects.
- encourage the learners to form the new letter combinations in sand, salt or flour, in the air, and on whiteboards and paper. If they can, encourage them to join the letters so that they have a fluent knowledge of what the letter pattern looks like, the sounds it represents and the feel of writing it.
- before the learners start each activity in the workbook, ensure that they know all the words, that they have already linked each word with the letter pattern needed to write it and that they fully understand what they need to do.

Introducing new ways of pronouncing known letter patterns

English is a complex language to read and spell; not only are there lots of ways of representing each sound, but there are often a variety of ways of pronouncing the letter patterns. The activities on pages 30–43 introduce some of these.

As before:
- always start from what is already known, so begin by revising the familiar pronunciations of the letter or letter pattern.

- start working orally, using pictures, objects and letter pattern cards, saying the sounds in words. Ask learners to sort pictures according to the vowel sounds. Then introduce the written forms of the words and discuss the different sounds made by the same letter or letter pattern.

Tricky words

Most sessions end with the introduction of associated tricky words. These words need to be learned but do not always follow phonic rules. Encourage the learners to try a 'phonics first' approach to tackling these words for reading and spelling. They should apply what they know and try to work out the word. As they do so, they will begin to see where they need to tweak certain letters or sounds.

Assessment

This workbook is cumulative, allowing learners to practise what they have previously learned. Use observations of the learner's progress to identify when a learner is struggling and, if necessary, revise activities both in the workbook and using your own resources.

In addition, there are revision pages at the end of every section. Use these to assess and monitor learning. Before you progress beyond a revision page, make sure that the learner can read all of the words and short texts.

Teaching using template 1

Template 1 is used on pages:

Page numbers	Phonics focus	Words to look out for
12–13	**/ee/** ee, ea	meal, leaves, leaning, reading, meat, peach, reach, beef, cheese, tree, sleep, feet, peel, sweets, sheep
22–23	**/ow/** ou, ow **/oi/** oy, oi	owl, frown, mouse, mound, cloud, house, shout, out coin, soil, join, enjoy, boy
30–31	Pronouncing **a** and **e**	(**a** like **day**) baby, alien, apron (**a** like **star**) giraffe, banana (**a** like **hot**) watch, swan (**e** like **sit**) bask<u>e</u>t, <u>e</u>leven, kitch<u>e</u>n
44–45	**/s/** **/z/**	horse, castle, basket, mouse, whistle ears, present, cheese, nose

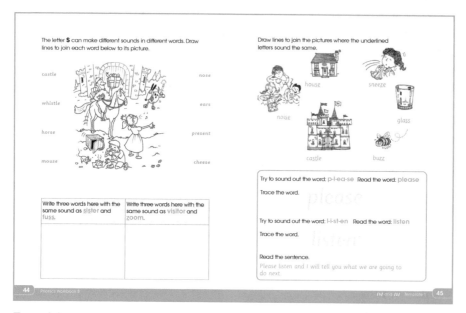

Teaching sequence

1 Read the instruction aloud to the learners. This is primarily a listening activity, not a writing one. Together, search for words that match the pattern given. Learners may identify words in addition to those shown above, or they may not find them all. Once you have identified words together, tell the learners to ring or label them as requested in the instruction. If there are words, as shown here, ask learners to read – or in some cases complete – the words, and join them to an appropriate part of the picture.

2 Read the instruction aloud to the learners. Before they start to draw or write, ask them to suggest a list of words that might be appropriate.

3 Read the instruction aloud to the learners. Again this is a listening activity where they are asked to identify words according

to their sounds. Ask learners to say the words aloud as they do the activity. It may be easier for them to work in pairs for this part of the activity.

4 This panel is used to introduce common words, often tricky words that cannot be read using phonics alone. Read the word aloud for the learners. Each time they finish writing the word over the letters shown, ask them to say the word aloud.

5 Read the sentence aloud to the learners. Ask them to follow with their fingers pointing to each word as you read it aloud. Remind the learners of the target word. Ask them to re-read the sentence with you, pointing to each word as they do so. Finally, ask them to re-read the sentence themselves, ringing the target words when they see them.

Teaching using template 2

Template 2 is used on pages:

Page numbers	Phonics focus	Words to look out for
8–9	Revision: **oi, ow, ar, or, ir, er**	shark, shirt, owl, star, coin, arm, skirt, car, cork
20–21	**/ar/** ar **/ir/** ur, er **/or/** aw, ore	bark, shark hurt, burn, bird saw, store, sport
32–33	Pronouncing **i** and **y**	lion, granny, child, lorry, pilot, baby
52–53	Spelling unstressed **/er/**	spider, sugar, whisper, trousers, fire, panda

Teaching sequence

1 Read the instruction aloud to the learners. Ask the learners to read the words in the central box aloud. Check that the vocabulary is familiar. Once the learners know the words, they should trace over them in this panel.

2 Identify the pictures. Make sure that the learners are familiar with the words. Once they have joined each word to its picture, ask them to sound out and copy the word in the box under each picture.

3 Read the instruction aloud to the learners. Together, name all of the pictures. Ask the learners to finish writing the words on the page. Suggest that they use the letter patterns from the previous page.

4 This panel is used to introduce common words, often tricky words that cannot be read using phonics alone. Read the words aloud for the learners. They should copy over the word, then write it independently along the line.

5 Read the sentence aloud to the learners. When you reach a blank, ask them which of the words in the box they would use to fill it. Let the learners work independently to fill the gaps.

Teaching using template 3

Template 3 is used on pages:

Page numbers	Phonics focus	Words to look out for
7	Revision of **ai**, **ee**, **ie**, **oa**, **oo**, **oo**	sheep, soap, paint, tie, bee, boot, foot
28–29	Revision	cake, tray, tree, leaf, bike, fly, light, pie, toe, bone, blow, coat, boot, glue, flute, bush, bird, cow, cloud, fire
38–39	**ow** cow, blow **ou** could, shoulder mouse, group	Words given
42–43	Revision	Words given
54–55	Revision	Words given

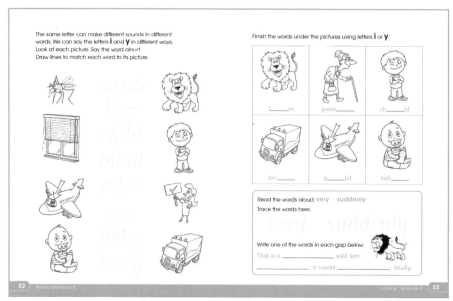

Teaching sequence

1 Sometimes the learners see pictures and have to write words here. On other pages, they are given words and are asked to draw the pictures. Read the instruction aloud to the learners. Make sure the words are familiar. Assess their learning and progress and identify any sounds or letter patterns that cause confusion.

2 This panel is not always present. It is used to introduce common words, often tricky words that cannot be read using phonics alone. Read the word aloud for the learners. Ask them to copy over the letters, then to write the word independently. Each time they finish writing the word over the letters shown, ask the learners to say the word aloud.

3 Read the instruction aloud to the learners. Ask them to look at each of the pictures, then to read each question aloud. The questions refer to the pictures. Learners should write 'yes' or 'no' after the question mark to answer the questions.

Teaching using template 4

Template 4 is used on pages:

Page numbers	Phonics focus	Words to look out for
5	Revision **sh**, **th**, **ch**, **ng**, **nk**	
6	Revision **ai**, **ee**, **ie**, **oa**, **oo**, **oo**	paint, sheep, bee, tie, soap, boot, foot
16–17	**/oa/** o_e, ow, oe	bowl, rainbow, goat, goal, nose, toe, open
26–27	**/f/** ff, ph **/w/** wh	dolphin, phone, coffee, cliff wheel, twins
34–35	**o** hot, cold, mother **u** hut, bush, super	piano, cola, octopus, glove pull, bull, superman
40–41	**c** cat, city **g** girl, giraffe	race, bicycle, pencil, circle dragon, bandage, giraffe
48–49	**/ai/** **/ee/** **/ie/** **/oa/**	crayon seat, happy, monkey night throw, window

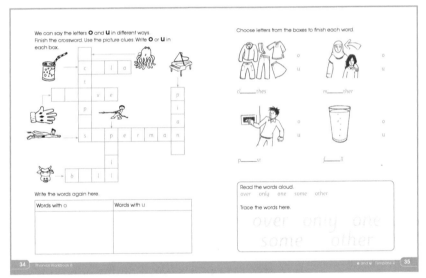

Teaching sequence

1 This panel is not always present. Say the sounds aloud and ask learners to repeat them with you. Learners can then trace the letter patterns on the page. Note that on page 16 the 'ow' represents the sound in 'slow' rather than in 'how'.

2 Read the instruction aloud to the learners. Ask them to identify the pictures. Ask the learners to work out what the missing letters are in each word. One letter should go in each box. Tell them to complete the page independently.

3 Read the instruction aloud to the learners. This is a sorting activity that asks the learners to separate the words according to sounds in the words.

4 Read the instruction aloud to the learners. Ask the learners to identify the pictures. Explain that they have to write letters to finish the words. Show them the boxes and tell them that they must choose from one of the choices in the box. Model completing the first word together, then leave the learners to finish the task independently.

5 This panel is not always present. It is used to introduce common words, often tricky words that cannot be read using phonics alone. Read the instruction aloud to the learners. Help them to read the words in the box. They should trace over each word, then write the words independently underneath.

Teaching using template 5

Template 5 is used on pages:

Page numbers	Phonics focus	Words to look out for
10–11	**/ai/** a_e, ay	cake, tray, tale, rain, came, tail
18–19	**/oo/** u_e, ue, ew **/oo/** u	soon, grew, blue took, put, bush
36–37	**ie** tie, field **ea** bead, bread	chief, field, thief, head, heavy, bread
47	**/sh/** and **/zh/** **/tch/** and **/dg/**	(ship) sheep, special, she (chip) creature, mixture, picture, adventure, chest (giant) strange, ages (pleasure) television, usual, treasure

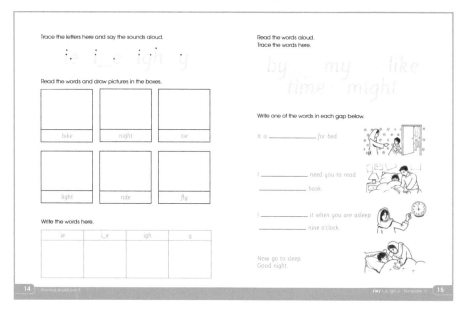

Teaching sequence

1 This panel is not always present. Say the sounds aloud and ask learners to repeat them with you. Learners can then trace the letter patterns on the page.

2 Introduce this short story. Make sure the learners know that they will need to read it aloud. They should be able to read all of the words in the story. Once they have read the story, the learners should identify and mark words as indicated.

3 Read the instruction aloud to the learners. This is a sorting activity, where they are asked to think about the sounds and letter patterns in the words they have marked.

4 Read the instruction aloud to the learners. Explain that the machine is a word-making machine – you feed it letters and it makes them into words. The learners' task is to predict which word the machine will make. The first

sound in the word is often underlined. Show the learners that each box of letters is numbered. They need to write their answer in the empty box with the same number on the opposite side of the sheet. Model working through the first of the words and show the learners where the answer is written. Give them time to work through the rest of the page independently.

5 This panel is used to introduce common words, often tricky words that cannot be read using phonics alone. Read the words aloud for the learners. Ask them to trace them on the page, then to write the words independently.

Teaching using template 6

Template 6 is used on pages:

Page numbers	Phonics focus	Words to look out for
4	**sh, th, ch, ng, nk**	cat, chin, ship, sink, king, swing
14–15	**/ie/** i_e, igh, y	bike, night, tie, light, ride, fly
24–25	**/air/** are, ear **/ear/** eer	stare, bear, chair, ear, deer, cheer
46	**/sh/** and **/zh/** **/tch/** and **/dg/**	Words given
50–51	**/oo/ /or/ /ir/ /ar/**	computer, walk, palm tree, earth, four, rescue, search, worm, daughter

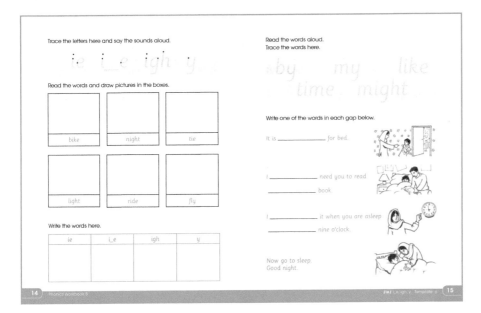

Teaching sequence

1 This panel is not always present. Say the sounds aloud and ask learners to repeat them with you. Learners should then trace the letters inside the outlines.

2 Read the instruction aloud to the learners. Ask them to identify the pictures. Encourage them to tell you the sounds in each word as they use 'phonic fingers' to show each sound. Support the learners as they use their phonics fingers to help them to think about each sound as they write it to spell the words.

3 This panel is not always present. Read the instruction aloud to the learners. Ask them to sort the words they have written in the table according to the sound in the words.

4 This panel is not always present. It is used to introduce common words, often tricky words

that cannot be read using phonics alone. Read the words aloud to the learners and talk about the letters in them. Ask them to write and say the words. Warn them that they will need to remember the words for the reading activity.

5 Read the instruction aloud to the learners. Tell them to read each sentence while they look at the picture. In some versions of the template, learners should use the common words to complete the sentences. In other versions of the template, there are no gaps but learners are asked to identify words with particular sounds which they are then asked to sort in a table at the foot of the page. Once you have completed the first sentence together, allow the learners to work independently to complete the activity.

Example words

Page	Letters and sounds	Useful words
10–11	**/ai/** a_e, ay	today, made, came, make, always
12–13	**/ee/** e, ee, ea	these, please, people
14–15	**/ie/** i_e, igh, y	by, time, like, my, might, high
16–17	**/oa/** oa, o_e, ow, oe	don't, old, so
18–19	**/oo/** u_e, ue, ew and **/oo/** oo, u	put, could, would, should
20–21	**/ar/** ar **/ir/** or, ur **/or/** or, aw, ore	are, your, were, saw, more
22–23	**/ow/** ow, ou **/oi/** oi, oy	about, our, enjoy
24–25	**/air/** are, ear **/ear/** ear, eer	there, their, dear, near
26–27	**/f/** ff, ph **/w/** wh	where, when
30–31	**a** **e**	what, want, ask, after
32–33	**i** **y**	find, child, very, yes, suddenly
34–35	**o** **u**	over, one, other, only, some
36–37	**ie** **ea**	friend, really, each, easy
38–39	**ow** **ou**	now, how, flower could, shoulder, trousers, group
40–41	**c** **g**	cat, city girl, giraffe
42–43	Revision	even, ever
44–45	**/s/** and **/z/**	please, listen
50–51	Revision and less common uses **/oo/ /or/ /ir/ /ar/**	early, earth, computer, walk, four, daughter, half